A Winter Walk

In *winter* WE LEAD
A MORE INWARD LIFE.
OUR *hearts* ARE
WARM AND CHEERY,
LIKE COTTAGES
UNDER DRIFTS, WHOSE
WINDOWS AND DOORS
ARE HALF CONCEALED,
BUT FROM WHOSE
CHIMNEYS THE SMOKE
cheerfully
ASCENDS.

Henry David Thoreau

A Winter Walk

AMERICAN ROOTS

Applewood Books
CARLISLE, MASSACHUSETTS

© 2014 Applewood Books

978-1-4290-9612-6

Cover and interior art from
Snowflakes: a Chapter from the Book of Nature (1863)

"A Winter Walk," by Henry David Thoreau, was first published in
the *Dial* in October of 1843.

Thank you for purchasing an Applewood book.
Applewood reprints America's lively classics—
books from the past that are still of interest to modern readers.
Our mission is to build a picture of America's
past through its primary sources.

To inquire about this edition or to request a free copy of
our current catalog featuring our best-selling books, write to:
Applewood Books
P.O. Box 27
Carlisle, MA 01741
For more complete listings, visit us on the web at www.awb.com

10 9 8 7 6 5 4 3

MANUFACTURED IN THE UNITED STATES OF AMERICA

The short works Applewood offers in its American Roots series have been selected to connect us. The books are tactile mementoes of American passions by some of America's most famous writers. Each of these has meant something very personal to me.

Applewood Books is located in an old candy factory on River Road in Carlisle, Massachusetts. Drive down our road a mile, and River Road becomes Monument Street in Concord, former home of Henry David Thoreau and the transcendentalists. At Applewood, we do our recycling and banking in Concord Center. However, just over the Carlisle line in Concord, halfway between our office and the town center, are the Punkatasset woods. There, I watch the seasons change, as I walk almost daily with my office companion and half-golden retriever, Dao Noi. We like winter best in these woods, Noi and I. Here, no doubt, Henry David Thoreau walked in winter. One day this past winter, after a walk, with Noi snoozing on my office couch, I reread this beautiful celebration of winter and walking.

> "*In winter we lead a more inward life. Our hearts are warm and cheery, like cottages under drifts, whose windows and doors are half concealed, but from whose chimneys the smoke cheerfully ascends.*"

ℚPhil Zuckerman

PUBLISHER

The wind has gently murmured through the blinds, or puffed with feathery softness against the windows, and occasionally sighed like a summer zephyr lifting the leaves along, the livelong night. The meadow-mouse has slept in his snug gallery in the sod, the owl has sat in a hollow tree in the depth of the swamp, the rabbit, the squirrel, and the fox have all been housed. The watchdog has lain quiet on the hearth, and the cattle have stood silent in their stalls. The earth itself has slept, as it were its first, not its last sleep, save when some street-sign or wood-house door has faintly creaked upon its hinge, cheering forlorn nature at her midnight work, the only sound awake twixt Venus and Mars,—advertising us of a remote inward warmth, a divine cheer and fellowship, where gods are met together, but where it is very bleak for men to stand. But while the earth has slumbered, all the air has been alive with feathery flakes descending, as if some northern Ceres reigned, showering her silvery grain over all the fields.

We sleep, and at length awake to the still reality of a winter morning. The snow lies warm as cotton or down upon the window-sill; the broadened sash and frosted panes admit a dim and private light, which enhances the snug cheer within. The stillness of the morning is impressive. The floor creaks under our feet as we move toward the window to look abroad through some clear space over the fields. We see the roofs stand under their snow burden. From the eaves and fences hang stalactites of snow, and in the yard stand stalagmites covering some concealed core. The trees and shrubs rear white arms to the sky on every side; and where were walls and fences, we see fantastic forms stretching in frolic gambols across the dusky landscape, as if nature had strewn her fresh designs over the fields by night as models for man's art.

Silently we unlatch the door,

letting the drift fall in, and step abroad to face the cutting air. Already the stars have lost some of their sparkle, and a dull, leaden mist skirts the horizon. A lurid brazen light in the east proclaims the approach of day, while the western landscape is dim and spectral still, and clothed in a sombre Tartarian light, like the shadowy realms. They are Infernal sounds only that you hear,—the crowing of cocks, the barking of dogs, the chopping of wood, the lowing of kine, all seem to come from Pluto's barn-yard and beyond the Styx;—not for any melancholy they suggest, but their twilight bustle is too solemn and mysterious for earth. The recent tracks of the fox or otter, in the yard, remind us that each hour of the night is crowded with events, and the primeval nature is still working and making tracks in the snow. Opening the gate, we tread briskly along the lone country road, crunching the dry and crisped snow under our feet, or aroused by the sharp clear creak of the wood-sled, just starting for the distant market, from the early farmer's door, where it has lain the summer long, dreaming amid the chips and stubble; while far through the drifts and powdered windows we see the farmer's early candle, like a paled star, emitting a lonely beam, as if some severe virtue were at its matins there. And one by one the smokes begin to ascend from the chimneys amidst the trees and snows.

The sluggish smoke curls up from some
    deep dell,
The stiffened air exploring in the dawn,
And making slow acquaintance with the
    day;

Delaying now upon its heavenward course,

In wreathed loiterings dallying with itself,

With as uncertain purpose and slow deed,

As its half-wakened master by the hearth,

Whose mind still slumbering and

 sluggish thoughts

Have not yet swept into the onward

 current

Of the new day;—and now it streams afar,

The while the chopper goes with step

 direct,

And mind intent to swing the early axe.

First in the dusky dawn he sends abroad

His early scout, his emissary, smoke,

The earliest, latest pilgrim from the roof,

To feel the frosty air, inform the day;

And while he crouches still beside the
    hearth,
Nor musters courage to unbar the door,
It has gone down the glen with the light
    wind,
And o'er the plain unfurled its
    venturous wreath,
Draped the tree-tops, loitered upon the
    hill,
And warmed the pinions of the early bird;
And now, perchance, high in the crispy air,
Has caught sight of the day o'er the
    earth's edge,
And greets its master's eye at his low
    door,
As some refulgent cloud in the upper sky.

We hear the sound of wood-chopping at the farmers' doors, far over the frozen earth, the baying of the house-dog, and the distant clarion of the cock. Though the thin and frosty air conveys only the finer particles of sound to our ears, with short and sweet vibrations, as the waves subside soonest on the purest and lightest liquids, in which gross substances sink to the bottom. They come clear and bell-like, and from a greater distance in the horizon, as if there were fewer impediments than in summer to make them faint and ragged. The ground is sonorous, like seasoned wood, and even the ordinary rural sounds are melodious, and the jingling of the ice on the trees is sweet and liquid. There is the least possible moisture in the atmosphere, all being dried up, or congealed, and it is of such extreme tenuity and elasticity, that it becomes a source of delight. The withdrawn and tense sky seems groined like the aisles of a cathedral, and the polished air sparkles as if there were crystals of ice floating in it. As they who have resided in Greenland tell us, that, when it freezes, "the sea smokes like burning turf-land, and a fog or mist arises, called frost-smoke," which "cutting smoke frequently raises blisters on the face and hands, and is very pernicious to the health." But this pure stinging cold is an elixir to the lungs, and not so much a frozen mist, as a crystallized midsummer haze, refined and purified by cold. The sun at length rises through the distant woods, as if with the faint clashing swinging sound of cymbals, melting the air with his beams, and with such rapid steps the morning travels, that already his rays are gilding the distant western mountains. Meanwhile we step hastily along through the powdery snow, warmed by an inward heat, enjoying an Indian summer still, in the increased glow of thought and feeling. Probably if our lives were more conformed to nature, we should not need to defend ourselves against her heats and colds, but find her our constant nurse and friend, as do plants and quadrupeds.

If our bodies were fed with pure and simple elements, and not with a stimulating and heating diet, they would afford no more pasture for cold than a leafless twig, but thrive like the trees, which find even winter genial to their expansion.

The wonderful purity of nature at this season is a most pleasing fact. Every decayed stump and moss-grown stone and rail, and the dead leaves of autumn, are concealed by a clean napkin of snow. In the bare fields and tinkling woods, see what virtue survives. In the coldest and bleakest places, the warmest charities still maintain a foothold. A cold and searching wind drives away all contagion, and nothing can withstand it but what has a virtue in it; and accordingly, whatever we meet with in cold and bleak places, as the tops of mountains, we respect for a sort of sturdy innocence, a Puritan toughness. All things beside seem to be called in for shelter, and what stays out must be part of the original frame of the universe, and of such valor as God himself. It is invigorating to breathe the cleansed air.

Its greater fineness and purity are visible to the eye, and we would fain stay out long and late, that the gales may sigh through us, too, as through the leafless trees, and fit us for the winter:—as if we hoped so to borrow some pure and steadfast virtue, which will stead us in all seasons.